Grand Country

The watershed of the Grand River is the geographically unifying and the economically sustaining force of Waterloo County. Flowing from the north near Elmira (right), collecting the waters of the Conestoga, Nith, and Speed rivers along the way, the Grand meanders by pastoral landscapes and rich agricultural lands before cascading over waterfalls where her power once fostered a thriving textile industry and now sustains the vibrant cities of Waterloo, Kitchener, and Cambridge. Waterloo County is truly "Grand" country.

"Crossed by 15 bridges and guarded by the spires of churches standing sentinel, the Grand River is the artery which links our past to our future as it shimmers serenely southward"
— Harry Currie,
Musician and Author.

Spring Tributary

Along the Blair Trail in southern Waterloo County, a spring-fed creek treks towards the Grand River (previous page).

IMAGES OF
Waterloo County

RICHARD BAIN

FOREWORD BY
PETER GZOWSKI

QUARRY PRESS

In Memory of Hugh

Horse's Gait
Spring blossoms surround a picturesque gate on John Street in the City of Waterloo (previous page), while at Doon Heritage Crossroads village (opposite) time has been turned back to 1914 when the pace of life was no faster than a horse's gait.

Foreword
BY PETER GZOWSKI

When I was a kid, and the world was simpler, Waterloo County was the centre of the universe. Peter John Gzowski Brown, I would scribble on the flyleaves of my schoolbooks (my mother, divorced from Harold Gzowski and remarried, having added my stepfather's surname to mine), Upper Duplex, 24 Park Avenue, City of Galt, Township of North Dumfries, County of Waterloo, Province of Ontario, Dominion of Canada, Continent of North America, Western Hemisphere . . . and so on to the limits of imagined space.

At the epicentre was Dickson Park, which stretched from beneath the bay window of our duplex across the road and down the hill toward the railway tracks and the river. The park, named, as was the stately stone school where I went when the park was quiet, for one of the county's pioneer families, was truly a land for all seasons.

In spring, as soon as the creeks in the surrounding countryside — creeks were *cricks* in Waterloo County, although the pants we wore all winter, baggy-thighed but laced tight at the knee (and patched with leather if you were lucky) were *breeks* — had begun to run with their cheerful rivulets of icy water, we took to the park for the first sessions of what we called tibby. Tibby, or tippy, as it may have been spelled, was the simplest of games: a long piece of broomstick for a bat; a shorter one to hit with it; two holes in the muddy ground, a cricket pitch apart, for wickets. We played it until the grass in the park was firm enough for baseball — flies and grounders, at first, and then, when the diamonds were ready, scrub, which is what we called the game other parts of the world knew as work-up.

There were two diamonds in Dickson Park. The more impressive, where the mighty Terriers played their Inter-county League games, was directly across the road from our duplex, its playing surface shielded from my bird's-eye view only by the tar-papered roof of its rickety wooden grandstand, from which, one spring, we dropped homemade bombs whose ingredients I never knew. The other, where we played our games of scrub and, later, more formal

Centre of the Universe

The Speed River, now banked by bicycle and hiking trails, was once the source of power for the mill industries in the former town of Hespeler (previous page). To the right is one of the original textile mills built in 1861 by Jacob Hespeler which has been home to American Standard since 1969.

The sound of children playing in the school yard of Dickson Public School (above) goes back to 1877 when the front door was first opened to students.

matches between schools, was at the farthest reaches of the Terriers' outfield, with the back of its batting cage turned to the barns that held livestock during the fall fair. Although the outfields of the two diamonds shared the open greensward, the park was large enough that, so far at least as I can remember, there were no occasions when fielders from different games were confused by simultaneous home-run clouts rolling past each other.

In summer, the Terriers were our heroes. The Inter-county League — I remember, I think, Galt, Kitchener (I told you Waterloo County was the centre of the universe), Brantford, Stratford, London, Ingersoll and St. Thomas, although I'm sure my list is incomplete and that there were others over the years — was perhaps Class C in a flourishing minor-league system that went all the way up to AAA. But in the days before television it seemed big-time to us. Like most minor-league clubs in those days, the Terriers were built around itinerant players who would slip into town and supplement their baseball incomes with jobs in the mills and foundries. Sometimes, indeed, these players even included people we'd heard of — Goody Rosen, for example, who'd had a stint with the AAA Toronto Maple Leafs, or, for part of one unforgettable season, Mickey Owen, who'd caught in the majors, even though he was best remembered for having dropped a third strike in the World Series. But our real heroes were the local boys who'd made good: Moth Miller, as quick as an antelope in the outfield, with his pants tucked in like plus-fours, running down every ball he could see, which, considering his Coke-bottle eyeglasses, was a remarkable percentage; Red Cupples on the mound (Red's younger brother Gordie pitched in our games at the other end of the park, for St. Andrew's school against Dickson), and, the greatest of them all, Wiggy Wylie at shortstop. Although I was never sure where Wiggy's nickname came from (he was Bill Wylie, though no one ever called him that), I imagined it was from the way he set himself at the plate, twitching his bat, and wiggling his hindquarters, for he not only played like a ballplayer, he *walked* like one, and for days after every Terriers game, we would shamble around our own diamond in emulation of his loose-limbed gait. "Are you *limping*," my mother asked one summer morning, as, my glove freshly rubbed with dubbin (dubbin worked on high-cuts in the winters, too), the crook of my arm already tanned a golden brown, I set off for the fields of play, proving, I suppose, that there were some things mothers — even those who lived across the road from the centre of everything that mattered — would never understand.

The fall had a magic of its own, not only in the yellows and crimsons of the hills and woods — for we were never far from the countryside — or the sense of renewal that filled the wine-sweet air, but in the life of the park as well. Almost as soon as school began, workmen raised goalposts on baseball's overlapping outfields, and marked the yards with stripes of lime for football, and the park was home to the red, blue and gold-clad champions of the GCI — and VS, of course, although the full title didn't fit the rhythms of our cheers. We essayed some football ourselves, touch, mostly, since we lacked the pads (if not the will) for tackle, and on one memorable occasion assembled a team of six park denizens to play a squad from Kitchener, with rules that said, except on a pass, two players had to touch the ball before it crossed the line of scrimmage. We won, somewhat to our own astonishment, thanks largely to a kid named Bob Keachie who could run like quicksilver, and we chanted the score — which comes to me now as Galt 10, Kitchener 5 (touchdowns in those days being worth only a nickel) — all the way home on the trolley. But the reason the game and its accompanying fanfare are still, for me, indelible, is more subtle than its outcome and, I'm afraid, more embarrassing.

A bunch of youngsters organizing something as adventurous as an out-of-town trip was, in those days, considered newsworthy in Galt, and one afternoon *The Reporter* — "The Rag," as we called it when it wasn't looking, though many of us earned pocket money by delivering it door to door — sent a photographer to pose us in the park. Without equipment, but with a boy's sense of drama, I decided to make myself look as tough as possible, and showed up for the photo session sporting Band-Aids across my nose and chin — badges, I hoped people would think, of some wounds of the game.

Even the thrills of football were set aside for the fall fair. For three magical days in September — though preparations began much earlier, under my watchful eye across the road — the park put on its autumn finery. A midway filled the baseball diamond and spilled over around the bandstand and onto our tibby pitch behind the backstop. Sheds and barns that stood unused for the rest of the year sprang to life. There were animals everywhere: sheep and pigs in pens along the hill; gleaming hunters and jumpers prancing around a show ring in front of the grandstand; sturdy Percherons and Clydesdales jingling with unaccustomed bells; sleek golden Jerseys and Guernseys and black and white Holsteins in their stalls. In the autumn air, the honkytonk of the midway barkers and the squeals of terrified rapture from the whirling rides mingled with the cries of roosters and the lowing of cattle, and the smell of candy-floss and frying hamburgers mixed with the sweet aromas of the barnyard.

Since long before I was lucky enough to move there, Galt had been an industrial city: a fortress, as was much of the county, of textile mills and furniture factories, of metal works and machine shops, symbolized,

Country Roads

Autumn colours blaze along
a country road near the
village of Ayr (above), while
the rural scene spreads out
panoramically near the
hamlet of Hawkesville
(next page).

in Galt, by the sprawling plant of the firm we called Babcock-Wilcox, Goldie and McCulloch-cox. The industrial age surrounded us, and supported many of our families (my own step-father was sales manager of the Narrow Fabrics Weaving and Dyeing Company Limited). But in the fall, when the fair came to Dickson Park, we were reminded of the richness of the landscape that was its setting, and of the variety and the ingenuity of the people who lived and worked along the county's tree-lined lanes and winding roads.

Winter was hockey, the most memorable season of all. After the midway had moved on to other counties and the farmers returned to the soil, boards would appear between the baseball backstop and the exhibition hall, outlining the setting of our winter dreams. Metal light-standards ringed the perimeter, and with the first ice our games would begin at dawn — or so it seemed — and last till only the fear of punishment sent us home. There was, to be sure, a smaller rink as well, for "pleasure skating" as the park would have it, but, in our view, for girls. On the *real* ice surface, we played forever, choosing up sides when the morning sessions began, amending the teams only to keep some semblance of equality as the day stretched on. Sometimes, in fact, there would be more than one game going on at the same time: one, for little kids, across the rink, one end-to-end between the snow-marked goals, and it was necessary to remember whose carved initials stood out in white on the puck you were supposed to be chasing. The rules were simple — no raising the puck, no body checking, no throwing your stick to bring down a fleeing breakaway — and our costumes and equipment simpler still: toques and breeks and sweaters (the Leafs and Red Wings being about equal in our favour), heavy stockings with — yes, magazines for shin pads (sometimes affixed by garters cut from inner tubes), hockey gloves for the well-to-do, sticks, with tar-taped blades that lasted until we wore them down to toothpicks.

One day, the world froze around us. Spring was approaching. An overnight rain had fallen on the deep blanket of snow. Then a snap freeze created what mountaineers call *verglas,* a thick but solid coating of ice on top of everything. At first we didn't notice what had happened. But when the first puck flew over the boards, instead of sinking into the snow it skittered off across crusted surface. The boy who took off after it stayed on top as well, sliding the puck ahead of him and calling with delight. The rest of us followed, pouring over the boards and taking to the open land, the puck soon forgotten. Across the baseball diamond we flew, over Red

Cupples' pitching mound and Wiggy Wylie's infield, and up the rise where I had posed in my unneeded bandages. For a while, we stayed on the hill, marking slalom courses with our up-turned hockey sticks and skimming among them like alpine skiers. But soon even that seemed ordinary. We took off again, climbing the park's weathered fence in our skates, sliding across Park Avenue, mounting the hill to Blair Road and off across the still-wintry fields, whooping and hollering as we went, as free as birds flying over the open land, moving in ever-expanding concentric circles from park to town to country, until, at last, we turned for home in the fading light.

I have thought, many times, of the metaphor of that joy-filled day.

As much as Dickson Park was our epicentre, we left it often. We took the trolley to Preston and Hespeler — skated, even (and with girls) on the rink behind the old Sulphur Springs Hotel. We hiked and rode our bikes among the surrounding pleasures: up Barrie's Cut, to Willow Lake and Puslinch, and through the Homer Watson landscape of Blair and Ayr and Doon. Later, and more adventurous, we rode as far afield as Kitchener and Waterloo, and my first memories of the Mennonites of the county's northern regions were from the seat of my shiny CCM. Even then, I realized there was a world beyond the park.

And, still later, there were other forces that matched the liberation of the *verglas*. When boyhood was over, so too was Galt, at least for me. My mother died. I moved to other galaxies.

Returning now, as I all too seldom do, I see the marks of progress everywhere. Galt itself, now folded into bustling Cambridge. Old street names swept away to avoid duplication with addresses in Hespeler and Preston. The murky river of my childhood returned to clean and sparkling life. At least one of the four banks that defined the corner of Water Street and Main now a chic restaurant. Many of the mills and foundries replaced by the humming prosperity of sophisticated technology — and one of them a restaurant too. Much of the countryside now scattered with subdivisions and shopping malls, with car-washes and fast-food franchises — the agricultural setting of my youth has given way to the growing, busy, modern world that Richard Bain has captured so eloquently in these pages. At Dickson Park, the outdoor rink has disappeared, its place taken by a modern, enclosed arena, and on the Saturday morning I drove by, kids as young as my grandchildren flopped from their parents' cars, with duffel bags full of equipment slung from their shouldered sticks.

Are there still Terriers, I wonder, though Wiggy Wylie has long gone? Do boys still play tibby in the spring?

Yes, I think, forever. Waterloo County, the centre of the universe, was a homeland. As these photographs make clear, it is one still, a place of people and memories, an anchor against the storms of change.

— PETER GZOWSKI
Spring, 1996

Frosted Scenes

The remains of the former Pattern Works Shop of the Canada Machinery Corporation in Cambridge (above) stand as a monument to an industrial golden age in Waterloo County. *Verglas* blankets fields south of Galt (next page).

Waterloo County Heritage

Built in 1853, "Woodside" was the boyhood home of Canada's 10th prime minister, William Lyon Mackenzie King (above). Maintained by Parks Canada, the house and grounds are open to the public for guided tours and festivities throughout the year.

The main parlour and dining room at Castle Kilbride (opposite), built in Baden in 1877 by James Livingston, have been restored to a splendour befitting James and his brother John, who formed J. & J. Livingston and ultimately became the owners of the largest linseed oil mill in Canada. In 1994 the Township of Wilmot moved its municipal offices into an addition constructed at the rear of the original home.

Doon Heritage Crossroads

A Dry Goods and Grocery Store has been reconstructed at Doon Heritage Cross-roads, and the "Old Petersburg Train Station" has been relocated to the site of this popular living museum.

Beer & Sausage

Behind the Blue Moon Tavern near Petersburg on the site of the old livery stables rests an historic beer wagon (above), which has been refurbished as an entertainment wagon for the annual Oktoberfest Parade celebrating the German heritage of Waterloo County.

The Joseph Schneider House (opposite), constructed in 1820, is the oldest surviving dwelling in Kitchener. A small settlement formed along Schneider's Road (Queen Street), which in time became the village of Berlin, renamed Kitchener (after British military leader Lord Kitchener) during the outbreak of the First World War.

Signs of the Times

Signs from the past and present
. . . Blair House Gifts (Blair),
Home Sweet Home (St. Jacobs),
Phillipsburg Corners, and
Reading Coal (St. Jacobs). EJ's
Restaurant and tavern in Baden,
built in 1874, is renowned for
its food and country hospitality.

*"Waterloo County is a destination
where visitors can experience a
blend of the old and the new,
urban and rural lifestyles. Our
history, culture, outdoor
experiences, and festivals entice
tourists from all over the world"*
— Jane Falconer,
General Manager,
*Kitchener-Waterloo Area Visitor
& Convention Bureau.*

Silos & Forges

The historic village of St. Jacobs is brimming with one-of-a-kind woollen and blacksmith shops, craft and antique stores, fine restaurants and quaint inns.

Spires & Shrines

The spire of St. Agatha
Catholic Church rises above
a century-old home
(opposite), and the Shrine of
Our Sorrowful Mother, St.
Agatha (above), is shrouded
in the morning mist.

The West Montrose Covered Bridge

The Covered Bridge at West Montrose, built in 1881, is the last remaining covered bridge in Ontario.

Mennonite Traditions

Originally set aside by the British Crown in 1784 as part of the reserve for the loyalist Six Nations natives, Waterloo County was settled by Mennonites from Pennsylvania during the early 19th century, giving the region a distinctive Germanic character.

Mennonite agricultural traditions have been preserved over the past two hundred years. Near Crosshill (previous page) farmers stook oats, and a fellow Mennonite ploughs straw stubble with a magnificent team of horses near Linwood (opposite).

Horse Power

A horse waits obediently outside the general store in Linwood (opposite), while two Mennonite mothers turn their heads from the camera (above). After church on Sunday morning (next page), a family drives home in a horse-drawn buggy, a familiar sight in northern Waterloo County.

Rites of Spring

Every spring the town of Elmira hosts the Elmira Maple Sugar Festival, attracting thousands of visitors over the course of a weekend. Over one half mile along main street is filled with booths selling and serving everything from sausage and sauerkraut to fresh baked apple fritters — and maple syrup, of course.

Farmers' Markets

The Waterloo Farmers' Market and Stockyard, located just south of St. Jacobs, is arguably the most famous in Ontario, rivalled only by the Kitchener Market in the core of the city, places where town and country folk meet to celebrate the harvest and forge a community.

Community Vitality

A day at the market raises
the spirits of young and old.

Market Square

Although the over 150,000 residents of the City of Kitchener have spread out from the old village of Berlin into handsome suburbs, Market Square remains the commercial and cultural heart of the community. Incorporated in 1912, the city was founded on the entrepreneurial skills of German immigrants who made Berlin and then Kitchener the pre-eminent industrial and manufacturing centre of the region.

Life Insured

The City of Waterloo is the life insurance capital of Ontario. Since issuing its first policy in 1870, The Mutual Life Assurance Company of Canada has become one of the largest life and health insurance companies in Canada. Their present offices on King Street in Waterloo consist of a unique blend of the old and the new. In 1912 the original building on this site was constructed, and in 1987 a 19-storey office tower was erected to grace the city skyline.

Berlin Monuments

The Canada Trust Centre in Kitchener is the regional office for mid-western and northern Ontario. Built in 1992, it is one of many new corporate offices making their home within the urban centre of Waterloo County. The clock tower from the "Berlin City Hall" now serves as a monument to the past in Victoria Park.

Municipal Halls

The Regional Municipality of Waterloo was established in 1973 through the amalgamation of Waterloo County with the "tri-cities" of Kitchener, Waterloo, and Cambridge (which in turn was created by the amalgamation of the communities of Galt, Hespeler, and Preston). The region now has a total population of over 400,000, making it the 12th largest municipality in Canada. Despite amalgamation, each community has retained a distinctive identity and political presence.

Cityscapes

The traditional architecture
of the old post office and the
majestic spire of Central
Presbyterian Church in
Cambridge (previous spread)
appear in harmony with the
modern skyline of Kitchener
(opposite), and the old
Grand River waterway in
Cambridge (right), now
transformed into a parkway,
offers a refreshing break
from the bustle of city streets
and highways.

Transformations

Langdon Hall in the village of Blair (above), built between 1898 and 1902, was the home of Eugene Langdon Wilks and his wife, Pauline Kingsmill, great granddaughter of Galt's founding father, William Dickson. William Bennett and Mary Beaton transformed the Hall into a five star country house hotel in 1987.

The former Victoria Public School (opposite), built in 1910, was converted into a community centre and housing complex for seniors and office for the Victoria Park Neighbourhood Association in 1993.

Historic Hotel

In 1836, at the corner of
King and Queen Streets in
Kitchener (right and
opposite), Frederick Gaukel
established an inn called
Gaukel's Hotel. In 1893
Abel Walper erected a four-
storey high, first-class hotel
with a tower on the site.
And in 1982 Fred Fontain
purchased the Walper
Terrace Hotel and began
restoring the building to its
Victorian splendour.

Glowing Light

The street lights at the corner of King and Queen in Kitchener cast a warm glow on the wall murals decorating the exterior of the buildings (opposite) like the stained-glass windows in the interior of St. Louis Catholic Church in Waterloo (above).

A winter sunset sets the snow aglow near the village of Roseville (next spread).

Bridges of Waterloo County

One of the many scenic bridges in the County, this historic trestle bridge (opposite) was constructed in 1879 by the Credit River Railway to span 1250 feet of the Grand River near Cambridge, bridging the city and the surrounding rural countryside (above and next spread).

Pastoral Bliss

Near Crosshill on a warm
August morning, the vision of
a solitary horse framed by a
fence covered with roses is
nothing less than idyllic, while
Rockway Gardens in
Kitchener (next page) is a
favorite spot to photograph
summer wedding celebrations.

Pastimes

Many peaceful hours can be passed near the tranquil pond at Victoria Park in the heart of Kitchener (opposite). Young fishermen angle along the banks of the Nith River at Kirkpatrick Park in the town of New Hamburg (above).

Waterloo Gardens

Brilliant showings of petunias and chrysanthemums surround the Oktoberfest Heritage Timeteller (above). The Mutual Life Assurance Company cultivates a stunning display of spring bulbs each year (opposite). This horticultural spirit also distinguishes the old residential neighbourhoods of Waterloo (next spread).

Public Places, Quiet Spaces

Speakers Corner in downtown Kitchener (below) offers a forum for public address, while the paths of Rockway Garden (opposite) provide the space for private thoughts.

The Hollyhock and the Ivy

Stalwart hollyhocks
complement the grey
stonework of many
Waterloo County country
shops (opposite). The ivy
begins to turn from green to
red on the walls of
Graystones Restaurant in
Cambridge (above).

Of Golf, Balloons & Polka

The Doon Valley Golf Club (previous page) nestled along the banks of the Grand River beside Highway 401 provides passersby with a sporting image of Waterloo County. Hot air balloons prepare for launching during the centennial celebrations for the Grand River Hospital and Kitchener Waterloo Health Centre (above). Grammy Award-winning polka artist Walter Ostanek (opposite) entertains at the opening ceremonies of the annual Kitchener-Waterloo Oktoberfest, the largest Bavarian festival in North America with over 600,000 people attending events.

Winter Sports

Young skaters take a break
for hot chocolate at the civic
rink outside of Kitchener
City Hall (opposite). The
Kitchener Rangers of the
Ontario Hockey League
have provided the region
with first class hockey since
1963 (below). Skiers make
their way to the top of the
hill at Chicopee Ski Club,
and a solitary hiker's track
leads into the woods near
Baden (next spread).

Cultural Life

The love of popular dance and band music in Waterloo County is rivalled by an appreciation for traditional dance and symphonic music. Dancers prepare for their annual recital "Get Up and Dance" at the Waterloo Dance Centre (above), and the Kitchener Waterloo Symphony, one of the leading orchestras in Canada, performs at The Centre In The Square, one of our finest concert halls (opposite).

"Nobody puts on airs here. On opening night, the corporate sponsor in his tuxedo is gladly seated next to the student in denim. Theatres need such audiences — people of imagination who are willing to become communities for an evening"
— Stuart Scadron-Wattles, Artistic Director, Theatre & Company, Kitchener.

"There's really nothing like the feeling of being part of a community of people who have come together to hear great music performed live"
— Chosei Komatsu, Conductor, Kitchener-Waterloo Symphony.

Christmas in Waterloo County

The people of Waterloo County celebrate the holiday season with a rich and reverent display of colour and good cheer. Castle Kilbride is always fully decorated for the festive season (opposite). The Festival of Lights in Waterloo Park can be seen from a horse-drawn sleigh (above). The shops of St. Jacobs delight passersby with elaborate window displays, and the Blue Moon Tavern in Peterburg is illuminated by the light of the moon, of course (next spread).

Home for the Holidays

The Waterloo studio of artist Peter Etril Snyder is decorated with murals depicting rural Mennonite life (above). A home in Baden appears to welcome family and friends (opposite).

Water Power

The Speed River cascades over a man-made waterfall in the old town of Hespeler (previous page), and the Grand River flows by the site of an old mill (right), now restored as a monument to the textile industry which provided a living for many Waterloo County residents.

"One of our major strengths is that so many successful companies are owned by local entrepreneurs who have a lifelong commitment to the community in which they raise their families. This is truly a place where families have opportunities to remain together for life"
— Valerie Gibaut,
*Director of Economic Development,
City of Kitchener.*

Shirts, Underwear & Beer

The original site of the John Forsyth Co. has been abandoned (opposite), marking the decline of one industry, but another founding industry, brewing and distilling, continues to thrive.

Established in 1984 by Jim Brickman, The Brick Brewing Company (above) follows in the tradition of the Kuntz brewery (now Labatt's) founded in Kitchener in the 19th century.

Oh What a Feeling

A new Toyota Corolla
undergoes final inspection at
the Toyota Motor
manufacturing facility in
Cambridge (above), the
largest of the many
automotive plants operating
in the region.

The Seagram Museum

Located on the site of the original Joseph E. Seagram distillery in Waterloo, The Seagram Museum (below) captures the growth of a community-based distillery into a multi-national industry, featuring a re-creation of a late 19th century barrel warehouse (next page).

Famous for Quality

Waterloo County is well-known as a meat-packing centre. Entering the region from the east along Highway 401 motorists see the familiar sign and clock of Schneiders meats, established in 1890 in the name of founding father J.M. Schneider.

Financial Security

Among the major fire and life insurance companies with head offices in Waterloo County are Manulife Financial (opposite) and Economical Mutual Insurance (next page), which has been serving customers since 1871 from a stately building on Westmount Road in Waterloo.

The Vocation of Innovation

Innovation and vocation are almost synonomous terms in Waterloo County, where schools like Galt Collegiate Institute and Vocational School (opposite) encourage the pursuit and application of ideas. A pressman checks the quality of the print in a copy of the *The Record* (above). Developer John A. ("Jack") Ball consults the engineer's plan with the foreman on the site of one of the many buildings Ball Brothers have constructed in the region (below), including Market Square in Kitchener.

"We are creating new ideas and concepts, turning them into reality before anyone else. We are almost living in the 21st century right now in this little part of Canada"
— Dr. Valentine O'Donovan, President, Com Dev Ltd.

New Offices for Old Industries

Babcock and Wilcox (above), Canada's largest manufacturer of steam generating products and services, started business in 1859 under the name of Goldie and McCulloch, but the name changed after Babcock and Wilcox became controlling partners in 1867.

KPMG's Cambridge offices are located in the Stonebridge Business Centre (opposite), formerly an aircraft school, machine shop, and navy school which operated during the Second World War.

Higher Education

Waterloo County is an education centre for Southwestern Ontario whose institutes of higher learning have gained international renown. The University of Waterloo (left) is Canada's largest school of engineering and features an innovative co-operative work-study program with industry. Established in 1957, the university now has a student population in excess of 18,000.

"Innovation and entrepreneurship, combined with prudent management, have characterized the Waterloo region since the early 19th century. The University of Waterloo was established by community leaders who saw that continued innovation required a university that would relate to industry. From these roots, it is easy to see how the university has played such a vital role in the transition to the 'new' knowledge economy"
— Dr. Douglas Wright,
Former President,
The University of Waterloo.

Contemplative Light

A glass tower on the University of Waterloo campus (opposite) reflects the daylight clouds. The Bell Tower atop Keffer Memorial Chapel (left) takes on a contemplative tone at dusk on the campus of Wilfrid Laurier University, renowned for music, business, and social science programs, while the John Aird Building on the Laurier campus (next page) is cast in haunting urban light.

"Laurier is all about people: our extraordinary students, our devoted faculty and staff, the many volunteers who serve on our Board of Governors and Advisory Boards, the citizens from surrounding counties who come to hear concerts, readings, and special lectures, the cheering crowds in University Stadium and at the Athletic Complex . . . our university is a setting, a challenge, an occasion, a resource and an opportunity"
— Dr. Lorna Marsden,
President & Vice-Chancellor, Wilfrid Laurier University.

Applied Arts & Science

In the robotics laboratory at The University of Waterloo (above) and the woodworking centre at Connestoga College (below), craft combines with technology, art with science.

Connestoga Wagon

On display at Connestoga College is a replica of the wagons used by early settlers travelling from Pennsylvania to Waterloo County (above), made by woodworking students who graduated from this scenic campus in 1971 (opposite).

The Spirit of the Place

A truly grand spirit pervades Waterloo County — in Millrace Park along the Grand River in Cambridge (left), in the fields of the Doon Valley (next spread), and in the misty waters and the unique suspension bridge near Luxembourg which a farming family uses to cross the Nith River during the spring run-off when the lane becomes submerged (following spread).

"Waterloo County shares a spirit embodied in all her citizens"

> — Dom Cardillo,
> *Former Mayor,*
> *City of Kitchener.*

A Haven for the Heart

Morning mist rises above the winter inhabitants of the Grand River (previous spread), a lone swan greets the day in a pond near Phillipsburg (left), and ducks feed at sunset in the Nith River at New Hamburg (next page).

Against the Storms of Change

"I moved to the area 20 years ago and was immediately impressed by the warmth of the people and the strong community spirit that binds them together. There is a small town charm that prevails. It is a wonderfully unique place . . . where else could you see a horse and buggy trotting along main street . . . where else does the main street run north, south, east, and west . . . where else do two streets cross each other three times in two different cities. Waterloo County has the best of all worlds. It is close enough to Toronto to take in a ball game or the theatre, but far enough away to preserve the charm of a county rich in heritage. If quality of life is what counts, there is no place I'd rather call home"

— Ron Johnston,
CKCO Television.

"The centre of the universe . . . a homeland . . . a place of people and memories . . . an anchor against the storms of change"

— Peter Gzowski

Acknowledgements

When I started photographing Waterloo County, I was struck by the diversity of the region, and by the generous spirit of those who call this wonderful place home. I was overwhelmed by the many offers of assistance from individuals, organizations, and businesses who all wanted to share in this pictorial tribute.

Epitomizing the willingness to contribute was Peter Gzowski, who shared his personal memories of his early years in Galt. To have the opportunity to collaborate with Peter was an honour, and I am indebted to him for his contribution. Two other individuals who assisted with their sound advice are Harry Currie and Philip Bast.

I was honoured by the contribution of a special group of citizens who provided their comments on the character of the region. Thanks to Ron Johnston, Chosei Komatsu, Valentine O'Donovan, Dom Cardillo, Jane Falconer, Valerie Gibault, Lorna Marsden, Doug Wright, Jack Bishop, and Stuart Scadron-Wattles, who have given so much of themselves to this community.

Others who assisted with this publication include John Ball, Greg Mordue, Sandra Couch, Rachel Smith-Spencer, Vic Degutis, John Morris, Glen Hepler, Paul Beam, Duane Donaldson, Arthur Stephen, Frank Emrich, Jim Quantrell, Karen Rosentral, Jim McInnis, Earl Evans, Mary McElwain, Marie Peacock, Lynn Rams, Ann Bennett, Jerry Dietrich, Brad Sparkes, Cheryl Bell, Laurie Schroeder, Pam Taylor, Kodak Canada, *The Record*, CKCO Television, The Waterloo County Board of Education, The Kitchener-Waterloo Symphony Orchestra, The Kitchener Rangers, The Transylvania Club Dancers, Toyota Canada, The City of Cambridge Archives, The University of Waterloo, Wilfrid Laurier Univerity, Connestoga College, Doon Heritage Crossroads, as well as the staff of Castle Kilbride and K-W Oktoberfest, and the students and staff of Dickson Public School.

Special thanks to Bob Hilderley and Susan Hannah at Quarry Press, who have created from a binder of photographs this book. It was great to work with such a professional and dedicated publisher.

Finally . . . my family. To my parents, Glen and Barbara Bain for their on-going support and for encouraging me to pursue my love of photography. To family who still live in Waterloo County. To Al and Joan Krische who spent most of their life in the County and gave me countless suggestions for photographs. And to Kelly, Caroline, and Daniel for their love and understanding.

To each and every one of you, as well as countless others, I thank you for helping in the publication of this book. Waterloo County has been enriched by your contribution.

Richard Bain

The publisher gratefully acknowledges the support of The Canada Council, Ontario Arts Council, and Department of Canadian Heritage in developing the art of writing and publishing in Canada.

Cataloguing in Publication Data

Bain, Richard (Richard G.), 1954-
    Images of Waterloo County

(Civic images)
ISBN 1-55082-152-0

    1. Waterloo (Ont : Regional municipality)--Pictorial works. 2. Waterloo (Ont. : Regional municipality)--History. I. Title. II. Series.

FC3095.W38B35 1996
971.3'44'00220 C95-900870-5
F1059.W32B35 1996

Design by Susan Hannah based on the work of Keith Abraham.

Colour separations by The LINOshop, Belleville, Ontario.

Printed and bound in Canada by Friesens, Altona, Manitoba.

Published by Quarry Press, Inc. P.O. Box 1061, Kingston, Ontario K7L 4Y5.